HOLY CITIES

ROME

Saviour Pirotta

Dillon Press
New York

First American publication 1993 by Dillon Press,
Macmillan Publishing Company, 866 Third Avenue,
New York, NY 10022

Macmillan Publishing Company is part of the Maxwell
Communication Group of Companies.

First published by Evans Brothers Limited,
2A Portman Mansions, Chiltern Street, London W1M 1LE

Printed in Hong Kong by Wing King Tong Co., Ltd.

10 9 8 7 6 5 4 3 2 1

Library of Congress Cataloging-in-Publication Data
Pirotta, Saviour
    Rome / Saviour Pirotta.
        p.   cm. – (Holy cities)
    Includes bibliographical references and index.
    Summary: A look at Rome as the spiritual center of the
Catholic Church and at the ceremonies and traditions of
Catholicism itself.
    ISBN 0-87518-570-3
    1. Rome (Italy) – Church history – Juvenile literature.
2. Catholic Church – Italy – Rome – Juvenile literature.
3. Vatican City – Juvenile literature.   [1. Rome (Italy) –
Church history.   2. Catholic Church. 3. Vatican City.]
I. Title. II. Series.
BX1548.R6P57 1992
263'.04245632 – dc20   92 - 19685

Acknowledgments

Editorial: Catherine Chambers and Jean Coppendale
Design: David English
Production: Jenny Mulvanny

Maps: Jillian Luff of Bitmap Graphics

The author and publishers would like to thank:

Dr. Marjorie Weekes, from the Pontifico Council
for Social Communication in the Vatican for
her help and advice.

Gordon Urquhart for all his advice and for the use of
his photographs.

For permission to reproduce copyright material the author
and publishers gratefully acknowledge the following:

Cover: Main photograph - Saint Peter's Church showing the
basilica - Gordon Urquhart; inset left - Pope John Paul II -
Rex Features; inset right - Swiss guards - Italian State Tourist
Board

Endpapers: Front - A view of the Vatican taken from one of
the many bridges that span the Tiber River - Gordon
Urquhart; Back - A view of the Vatican at sunset when the
church bells ring the *Angelus* - Gordon Urquhart

Title page: Statues on the front of San Giovanni in Laterano -
Gordon Urquhart

Contents page: For hundreds of years, pilgrims visiting Saint
Peter's Church have stopped to kiss the bronze foot of Saint
Peter's statue. Many people believe that this act of humility
washes away some of their sins. On June 29, which is the
feast of Saint Peter and Saint Paul, the statue is dressed up
like a Pope - Gordon Urquhart

Page 6 - Zefa; page 7 - Bernard Van Berg, The Image Bank;
page 8 - Gordon Urquhart; page 9 - (top) Gordon Urquhart,
(bottom) Travel Photo International; page 10 - (top) Gordon
Urquhart, (bottom) e.t. archive; page 11 - James H. Morris;
page 12 - Gordon Urquhart; page 13 - Gordon Urquhart;
page 14 - (top) Gordon Urquhart, (bottom) Ronald Sheridan,
Ancient Art & Architecture Collection; page 15 - Gordon
Urquhart; page 16 - Gordon Urquhart; page 17 - Italian State
Tourist Board; page 18 - Gordon Urquhart; page 19 -
Topham Picture Source; page 20 - (left) Gordon Urquhart,
(middle) Topham Picture Source; page 21 - Gordon
Urquhart; page 22 - Gordon Urquhart; page 23 - Gordon
Urquhart; page 24 - Gordon Urquhart; page 25 - Gordon
Urquhart; page 26 - Gordon Urquhart; page 27 - Travel
Photo International; page 28 - Gordon Urquhart; page 29 -
Gordon Urquhart; page 30 - Gordon Urquhart; page 31 -
Gordon Urquhart; page 32 - Ronald Sheridan, Ancient Art &
Architecture Collection; page 33 - (top) Ronald Sheridan,
Ancient Art & Architecture Collection, (bottom) Gordon
Urquhart; page 34 - (left) James H. Morris, (right) Gordon
Urquhart; page 35 - James H. Morris; page 36 - Gordon
Urquhart; page 37 - Robert Harding Picture Library; page 38
- Gordon Urquhart; page 39 - Gordon Urquhart; page 40 -
(top) Topham Picture Source, (bottom) James H. Morris;
page 41 - Topham Picture Source; page 42 - (top) Popperfoto,
(bottom) Gordon Urquhart; page 43 - (top) Topham Picture
Source, (bottom) Gordon Urquhart; page 44 - (top) Gordon
Urquhart, (middle) Topham Picture Source, (bottom)
Gordon Urquhart.

Contents

Introduction

Rome, the capital of Italy, has always been a holy city, and sometimes a very powerful one. It was built on the famous Seven Hills around the Tiber River. Rome was once the center for the worship of ancient gods. Now it has at its heart a tiny separate state called the Vatican. This is the center of the largest Christian religion in the world: the Roman Catholic Church.

Many thousands of people come to Rome every year as pilgrims. They come to pray in its churches and most of all they visit the Vatican, where they can take part in religious celebrations and perhaps see the Pope, the leader of the Roman Catholic Church.

There is a row of columns on either side of Saint Peter's Square. They symbolize the Catholic Church as it embraces the world. ▼

Before you begin

When we use numbers, we usually write them down like this: 1,2,3, and so on. These numbers are called Arabic numerals. Sometimes numbers are written differently. These numbers were developed by the Romans and are called Roman numerals.

You will find some of these numbers in this book. This table will help you to find out what they mean.

Roman	Arabic	Roman	Arabic	Roman	Arabic
I	1	XI	11	XXI	21
II	2	XII	12	XXII	22
III	3	XIII	13	XXIII	23
IV	4	XIV	14	XXIV	24
V	5	XV	15	XXV	25
VI	6	XVI	16	XXVI	26
VII	7	XVII	17	XXVII	27
VIII	8	XVIII	18	XXVIII	28
IX	9	XIX	19	XXIX	29
X	10	XX	20	XXX	30

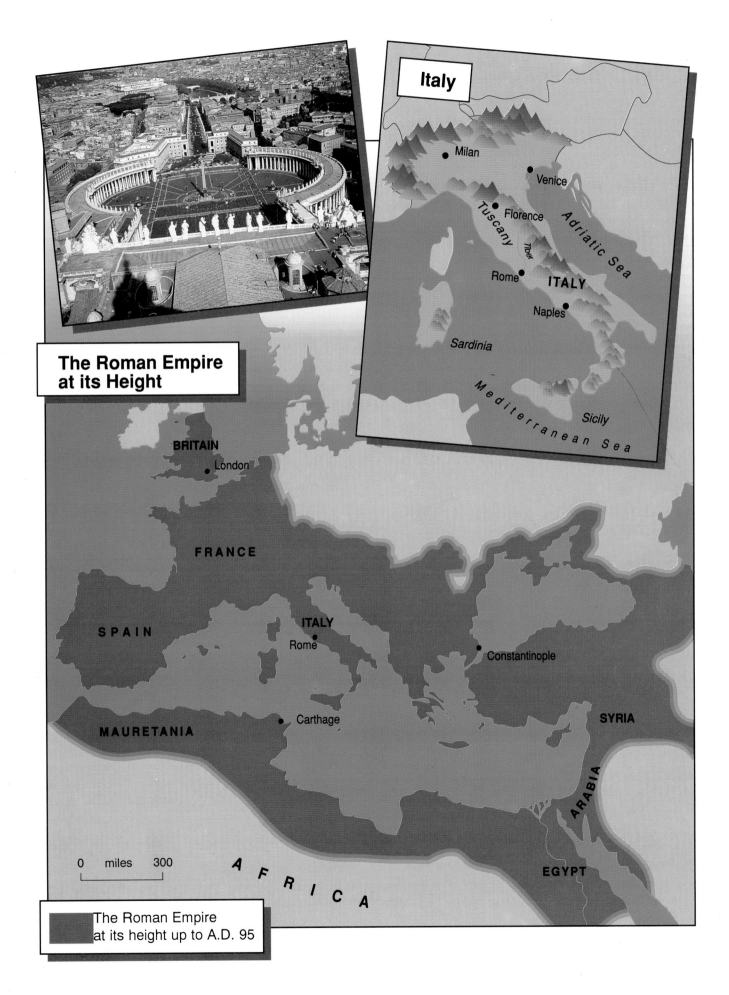

The Roman Empire
at its Height

Italy

Milan

Venice

Tuscany

Florence

Tiber

Adriatic Sea

Rome

ITALY

Naples

Sardinia

Mediterranean Sea

Sicily

BRITAIN

London

FRANCE

SPAIN

ITALY

Rome

Constantinople

MAURETANIA

Carthage

SYRIA

ARABIA

0 miles 300

A F R I C A

EGYPT

The Roman Empire
at its height up to A.D. 95

The birth of Rome

The city of Rome was founded over 2,700 years ago. Its official birthday is April 21 and its first king was Romulus. According to legend, Romulus and his twin brother, Remus, were the children of the god Mars. When they were babies, their earthly father, the wicked king Amulius, left them on the bank of the Tiber River to die. Luckily, a shepherd saw them sucking milk from a mother wolf on Palatine Hill and saved them.

When they grew up, Romulus and Remus decided to build a city on Palatine Hill. But they quarreled and fought. Remus was killed and Romulus became the king of the city, developing it on the Seven Hills on which much of Rome still rests.

There is another legend that the three local tribes of Ramnes, Tities, and Luceres joined together under King Romulus to become the first inhabitants of Rome. But the ancient ruins on Palatine Hill tell us a different story. They reveal an ancient burial ground, the Lapis Niger, which is believed to be the grave of Romulus. They also show that although people did live in tribes among the hills more than 3,000 years ago, they were probably the local Latin, Roman, and Sabine peoples, who lived in scattered communities.

As a city, Rome did not develop until the 6th century before the birth of Christ (B.C.). The Etruscans from Tuscany, to the north of Rome, conquered the local peoples and organized the scattered villages into a city. The Etruscans drained the marshy valley between the Capitoline and Palatine hills and built on it an enormous marketplace. This was later known as the Roman Forum and is now one of the most important landmarks of ancient Rome. They also built a huge

◀ *This statue of a wolf stands on top of the Capitoline Hill above the Roman Forum. It was made by the Etruscans in the 6th century B.C. The twins were added in 1510.*

The Roman Forum was a marketplace surrounded by important buildings such as the law courts and the Curia, where government officials met to discuss affairs of state. The remains of smaller forums can be seen in other parts of the city. ▶

The Colosseum was a massive sports arena. Its remains show the ancient Romans' great building and engineering skills. It used to seat 50,000 people and had an amazing system of shades to shield the spectators from the sun. During its opening ceremony, which lasted over 100 days, some 5,000 animals and many gladiators were killed. Every Good Friday there is a ceremony held in the Colosseum to honor the early saints who were thought to have been killed there.

wall around the communities living on the Palatine and Capitoline hills. Their **frescoes** lined the walls of large tombs, and they built temples for their gods. The Etruscans made many beautiful works of art and jewelry in bronze and silver. In 509 B.C. the Etruscans were defeated in battle by the local Romans, who took over the city.

Rome expands

Rome was built very near the sea, on the west coast of what is now Italy. It grew from a small town into a powerful city because its position was on a good crossing point on the Tiber River. Once a bridge was built, traders and travelers could cross the river easily. Businesses and settlements developed.

After the Romans took over, the city of Rome expanded quickly. Ideas about ruling such a vast city also grew. Its rulers made Rome into a spiritual center as well. They filled it with temples dedicated to their

▲ The famous Arch of Constantine is decorated with sculptures and details taken from other temples. It was built in A.D. 315 to celebrate Constantine's victory over Maxentius.

This thick marble ▶ column was built by Emperor Trajan, who was also a famous military leader. It stands about 100 feet high and there are 2,500 separate figures carved on it. They were once painted in bright colors.

◀ An Etruscan pot made in the shape of a woman's head

Roman gods and built a Pantheon, a temple for all the gods in the world.

Today, we can still see traces of the city's grand past among the buildings of modern Rome. The Pantheon, ever glorious, is still there, and even though they are in ruins, monuments like the Circus Maximus, the Colosseum, and the Roman Forum prove that ancient Rome must once have been the most splendid city the world has ever seen. Its **civilization** and government became models for many other countries long after Rome had lost its power.

The Romans took over many other cities that had been developed by the Etruscans and eventually built an empire, which for 800 years ruled much of Europe, North Africa, and parts of Asia (see map on page 7). The Roman Empire slowly lost its strength and was finally weakened in the 5th century A.D. after several invasions from Northern Europe and North Africa.

Key words

frescoes paintings on walls, made on damp plaster

civilization the culture of a particular people: their art, architecture, writings, way of dressing, cooking, dancing, etc.

A.D. *Anno Domini:* the years after the birth of Christ

The Colosseum

One of the most outstanding examples of Roman architecture, the Colosseum was the major center of entertainment in ancient Rome. Construction began under Emperor Vespasian (A.D. 69 – A.D.79) and ended in A.D. 80. Shaped like a football stadium, the four-story structure is 161 feet high, 600 feet long, and 500 feet wide. At one time, the Colosseum could be sealed off and flooded so that mock sea battles could be held there.

The early Christians come to Rome

Trouble in Judea

Not everyone in the ancient world admired Rome and what it stood for. Many nations, especially those conquered by its armies, detested it. Their peoples refused to pay taxes to the Roman ruler, and they did not want to obey Roman law or worship Roman gods.

Among these rebellious peoples were the Jews. The Jews prayed to their one God, for they did not believe in the many gods of the Romans. For a long time, these people of Judea had been expecting a Messiah, a leader or champion, who would free them from their Roman captors. They prayed every day for the coming of this savior.

According to the Bible, the man who came was not a political or military leader come to save the Jews from the Romans. Instead he

▲ These tomb carvings show scenes from the life of Christ. The early Christians were buried in underground caves called catacombs. Here they also held a service to celebrate the dead person's reunion with Jesus in heaven.

◀ Although Saint Paul never met Jesus, he was responsible for spreading his teachings to many countries. Paul was beheaded in Rome. Today a magnificent church stands over his grave.

had come to show the Jews how God wanted them to live. This man was known as Jesus of Nazareth. Even though he came in peace, the Roman rulers in Judea and some Jewish leaders still saw Jesus as a threat to their power.

Jesus of Nazareth

Christians believe that Jesus is the Son of God. He was born in Bethlehem nearly 2,000 years ago and lived most of his life in the small town of Nazareth. His mother's name was Mary, and his earthly father was a carpenter named Joseph.

Jesus himself became a carpenter, but just after his 30th birthday, he set out to bring the word of God, his heavenly Father, to the people. He chose twelve men to be his special **disciples**. Simon the fisherman was selected to be their leader. Jesus renamed him Peter, which means "rock." Jesus said, "You are Peter, and on this rock I will build my church." After Jesus' death, Peter was made

the first bishop of Rome. He became known as the Pope, the holy father and head of the Roman Catholic Church.

Every day Jesus preached to his followers. He told them he had come to save them from their sins. Sometimes Jesus performed miracles. He told them that they would go to God's **eternal** kingdom in heaven if they loved their fellow men and obeyed his laws.

Some Jews believed that Jesus was the Messiah they had been waiting for. Other Jews, and Herod, a local ruler who had been given power by the Romans, did not like this. Herod and the Roman governor of Judea, Pontius Pilate, felt that they had a troublemaker on their hands.

Jesus Christ was then arrested and sentenced to death by **crucifixion**. His followers put his body in a stone tomb. But Jesus rose from the dead three days later and appeared before his disciples. He then ascended to heaven to be with his Father, God. This is the basis of the Christian faith.

A few months later, Christ's followers started to travel the world preaching his teachings. Peter and another new Christian named Paul went to Rome, the center of the worship of the Roman gods. They formed a small Christian community there. Rome was a dangerous place for Christians. But as Rome was the center of a large empire, Christianity soon spread to many other parts of Europe, Asia, and North Africa that were under Roman control.

The martyrs

The Romans were not at all pleased to see Christians in their city. The followers of Jesus refused to worship Roman gods or to become soldiers in the Roman army. They were blamed for everything that went wrong in the city, including the burning of Rome in A.D. 64.

The Roman emperors passed laws that made it illegal to be a Christian. Anyone caught praying to Jesus, or to his mother Mary, was put to death. Paul was beheaded

▲ Saint Peter, like many other Christians and political prisoners, was held in the Mamertine Prison close to the Roman Forum. Behind the gates there is a horrible dungeon with no doors or windows. Prisoners were thrown inside it from a hole in the roof. In 1598, a small church was built over it. It is called Saint Joseph of the Carpenters.

▲ *This picture decorating a woman's tomb shows that the early Christians prayed with their hands held up high.*

in a dark prison cell. Peter was crucified upside down in Emperor Nero's circus. This was a large arena rather like a football stadium. The spectators sat on stone seats rising high above the ring in the center. The vast crowds were entertained not only by games and feats of strength, but also by cruel punishments for those out of favor with the emperor.

But the Christians would not give up. They buried Peter on Vatican Hill, and a small **shrine** was built over his grave. A man named Linus was chosen to become the next Christian leader. His followers continued to practice their religion in secret until, many years later, during the reign of Emperor Constantine from A.D. 312 to A.D. 337, Christians were allowed to worship openly. How Constantine came to allow free worship can only be described as a miracle.

Constantine's vision

Constantine did not become emperor of Rome easily. He had to fight other leaders who wanted power. Before a battle with one of his enemies, Maxentius, Constantine had a vision. He saw a cross, the symbol of Christianity, appear in the midday sky. The cross had a message written on it in Greek. It said: "By this, conquer!" Constantine did indeed defeat Maxentius, and he finally took over the Roman Empire.

Constantine's vision was of great importance to the Christians in Rome, for the emperor had great sympathy for them. He allowed Christians to worship openly in A.D. 313, and he built a great church, or basilica, over the shrine of Saint Peter.

Constantine himself did not become a Christian until just before he died, and Christianity did not become the official religion of Rome until A.D. 380. The Pantheon was made into a church in A.D. 608.

A different kind of Rome

Although Constantine gave a lot to Christianity, his reign brought to an end the great power of Rome as the capital of the Roman Empire. He no longer saw Rome as the center of his vast empire. Instead, he

▲ *The face of the Emperor Constantine was stamped on many Roman coins. Although he allowed Christians to worship openly, Constantine did not lead a Christian life. He worshiped the gods Sol and Apollo.*

▲ As a result of persecution early Christians had to use secret symbols. The one above stands for Christ. It was carved on tombs to show that Christians were buried inside. Another popular symbol for Christ was the fish.

This fresco depicts a miraculous story from the life of Saint Clement, the fourth Pope. According to legend, a noblewoman named Theodora used to secretly visit the catacombs to worship. One day her jealous husband, Sisinnus, followed her. As punishment for his jealousy, Sisinnus went blind and deaf. Later, Saint Clement is thought to have restored his sight and hearing. ▼

looked eastward to the ancient city of Byzantium, now in modern Turkey. He renamed the city Constantinople in A.D. 330 and ruled the empire from there until his death in A.D. 337. Even many Roman officials moved out of the city to Milan, far north of Rome.

But many Christians, including the leaders of the Christian Church, remained in Rome. They felt they had to be close to the many places where the first Christians were **martyred** for their faith. They had to look after the pilgrims that came to visit the shrines to those first Christians, and Saint Peter's grave. Rome became a different kind of spiritual center: a Christian one. People were drawn to Rome even though it no longer was a great empire. They saw Rome as the cradle of what became the Roman Catholic Church, often known just as the Catholic Church.

Key words

disciples men chosen by Jesus Christ to follow him and who later spread his teachings

eternal something that lasts forever; having no end

crucifixion killing someone by hanging them on a large cross, nailing their hands and feet to it

shrine a place, visited by pilgrims, where holy people are thought to have lived or died

martyr someone killed for what she or he believes in

A.D. and B.C.

In 532, a monk named Dionysius Exiguus began the system of dating years using A.D. and B.C. He called the year in which he believed Christ was born A.D. 1. A.D. means anno Domini (in the year of our Lord). Any year before A.D. 1 was called B.C. (before Christ).

The Vatican

Over the centuries the Popes built a huge and powerful organization to run the Catholic Church, which had spread to many countries. But by the 19th century their power had been taken away by the rulers of Italy. However, in 1929, the Italian dictator Mussolini gave Pope Pius XI a tiny state, which is actually a little city within Rome itself. It is governed by the Pope and senior Church leaders and has become the powerful center of the largest Christian Church in the world. This city-state is called the Vatican.

The Vatican State today

The Vatican is the smallest state in the world. It measures less than .2 square miles and is completely surrounded by the rest of Rome (see map on page 17). Its population is only 500. There is a high wall all around it, but no one needs a passport to enter. Most big countries have an embassy there.

Although it is small, the Vatican State has its own bank, post office, and train station. It also publishes its own newspaper. This is called *L'Osservatore Romano*, or *The Roman Observer*. It was first published in July 1861.

The Vatican Bank is commonly known as *Il Banco Dello Spirito Santo*, or the Bank of the

Holy Spirit, and it has branches all over Rome. The post office is situated in Saint Peter's Square. It sells its own stamps, which are collected by people all around the world.

The train station is used only once a day. A small train brings in goods to be sold to people working in the Vatican.

The Vatican also has its own radio station. It was the very first radio station in the world. Its huge antennas outside Rome transmit religious programs worldwide.

The Vatican Palace

The largest building in the Vatican State is the Vatican Palace. Most of it was built in the 15th century. It is really a collection of different buildings, courtyards, and gardens that together cover an area of 68,750 square yards. There are about 1,400 halls and chapels and 11,000 rooms within its walls. The Pope and his staff live and work in only a very small number of them. The rest are used for the Vatican museums and a library.

The museums have the largest collection of ancient works of art in the world. Crowds of

▲ *The Vatican's own newspaper is published every day in Italian. A shorter editon in other languages is on sale once a week.*

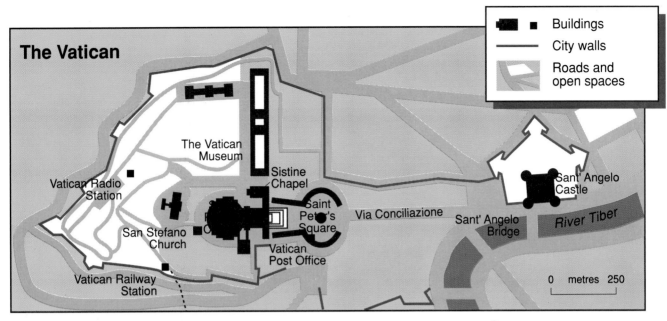

The Vatican

Legend:
- Buildings
- City walls
- Roads and open spaces

The Vatican Museum

Sistine Chapel

Saint Peter's Square

Vatican Radio Station

San Stefano Church

Vatican Post Office

Vatican Railway Station

Via Conciliazione

Sant' Angelo Bridge

Sant' Angelo Castle

River Tiber

0   metres   250

◄ *The Vatican Museum is the largest in the world. It has 13 separate galleries that altogether are 10 miles long. There are so many things to see that visitors choose different routes around it to see what they want. The shortest route takes three hours.*

visitors come to see them every day. As there is too much to take in during one visit, the **curators** have helpfully divided the museums into different sections. Two of these are the Egyptian section with its mummies and **sarcophagi** and the Museo Chiaramonti, which is full of Etruscan works of art.

The Pope's personal guards are called the Swiss Guards because they were brought to the Vatican from Switzerland by Pope Julius II. They formed part of the Vatican army. Their colorful uniforms were designed in the 16th century. Their weapons, known as halberds, are just for decoration. ▼

Key words

curators people who look after museums and galleries

sarcophagi tombs, often of carved stone

A troubled past

The hill on which the Vatican stands was once the site on Roman emperor Nero's public gardens and his infamous circus, where many Christians were killed by wild animals as entertainment for the emperor and his court. The founders of the Vatican built the city there because it is believed that Saint Peter was crucified on the hill and buried nearby.

The Pope

A spiritual guide

Saint Peter was the first bishop, or Pope, of
Rome. Today's Pope is the leader of the
Catholic Church and lives in the Vatican,
surrounded by his advisers. The Pope's job is
to guard and protect the unity of the Catholic
Church. He also acts as a spiritual leader to
the millions of Roman Catholics around the
world. His role has been compared with that
of a good shepherd who looks after his flock
and leads it safely to the fold.

Bishops look after a group of churches and
their **congregations**. The Pope chooses the
bishops who are thought to follow the
instructions of the first **apostles**. Sometimes
the Pope writes special letters to the bishops.
These letters are called encyclicals and they
explain the Catholic Church's point of view
on matters of faith. They are sent out to every
parish in the world.

*This carving of the Pope's coat of arms is found above
Saint Peter's Church. The headdress has three crowns
and the keys represent the Pope's power to open the
kingdom of heaven.* ▼

Urbi et Orbi: to the city and to the world

Every Sunday the Pope talks to the crowds in Saint Peter's Square from a window in his palace. He usually makes a short speech, which the people listen to carefully. During big festivals, such as Christmas and Easter, the Pope blesses the whole of the Catholic Church and his message is broadcast worldwide on radio and television. The Pope's Easter blessing is known as *Urbi et Orbi*. The name of the blessing is in Latin, the traditional language used by the Catholic Church and spoken by the ancient Romans. But the Pope broadcasts his message in many different languages.

▲ *Pope John Paul II addresses the world at Easter and gives his special blessing in more than twenty languages.*

The councils

On fourteen different occasions, the Popes have called all the bishops of the world to Rome. They came to discuss urgent and important matters. The first of these meetings, called General Councils, took place in 1123. The last, called by Pope John XXIII and named the Second Vatican Council, started in 1962 and finished in 1965. Pope John wanted the Catholic Church to face the problems and realities of the modern world. He called the Council to discuss with his bishops how the Church could modernize in the 20th century (see page 42).

Until now, there have been 263 Popes. Most of them have been Italian. One, Adrian IV, was English. The present Pope, John Paul II, is Polish.

Electing a new Pope

When a Pope dies, a new one is elected right away. The cardinals, who are the chief advisers to the Catholic Church, lock themselves in the Sistine Chapel and start a secret ballot, or vote. This is called a "conclave." It is not easy for the cardinals to elect a new Pope. The selected man must have more than two thirds, or a majority, of votes. The election process usually lasts from fifteen to twenty days. In theory, any Catholic man in the world can become Pope but in modern times, the cardinals have chosen from among themselves.

Every time the votes are counted, the ballot papers on which the votes are made are burned, and the smoke is allowed to escape from the Sistine Chapel. Crowds gather in Saint Peter's Square to watch the smoke closely. If it is black, they know that the ballot has been unsuccessful. But white smoke shows that a new Pope has been elected.

▲ *When a Pope is being elected, people watch the chimney on the Sistine Chapel roof to see if the ballot has been successful.*

The cardinals are the Pope's advisers and are selected personally by him. They are known as "The College." When the Pope dies the cardinals elect a new one. ▶

Then the Camerlengo, the master of ceremonies, calls out from a balcony in Saint Peter's: "*Habemus Papam,*" which means, "We have a Pope." The news is immediately transmitted all over the world by radio and television.

The room of tears

The new Pope is led into a special room to change from his old robe into a new, white one. This special room is called "The Room of Tears" because here the new Pope must take on the burdens of the world. He has already left his own personal life behind and dedicated the rest of his days to the Catholic Church. Next, the new Pope selects a new name. Then he steps out on to a balcony in Saint Peter's Church and blesses the waiting crowds for the first time.

Not all the Popes throughout the centuries have been popular. Some have not even

▲ Portraits of the 263 Popes decorate this frieze in the church of Saint Paul's Outside the Walls. The church was given its name because it was built outside the old city of Rome. According to an ancient legend, the world will come to an end when all eight remaining frames are filled.

appeared to follow the teachings of Christ. Others have tried to gain riches and power or have supported cruel rulers of other states. The actions of some Popes have led to divisions within the Catholic Church.

Still, this has never stopped millions of Catholics from seeing the Pope, and Rome, as the center of their faith on earth.

Key words

congregation people attending a particular house of worship or service

apostles Christ's twelve special disciples, later known as the apostles, or the men who spread Christ's teachings

parish the whole area around a church, and the church itself, looked after by the priest of the church

What's in a name?

When a person is elected Pope, he chooses a new name. What are the most popular names for Popes? There have been 23 Johns, 16 Gregorys, 15 Benedicts, 14 Clements, and 13 Leos and Innocents.

An audience with the Pope

Every Wednesday morning the Pope meets some of the many pilgrims who come to Rome from around the world. Sometimes this meeting, called an "audience," is held in Saint Peter's Church itself. But generally it takes place in a modern hall built especially for the purpose. This is called the Hall of Paul VI and is situated inside Vatican City.

The audience does not start until eleven o'clock in the morning, but people begin gathering outside Saint Peter's much earlier. They all carry special passes that allow them to make their way to the audience hall.

Viva Il Papa

At eleven, the Pope makes his entrance. As he mounts the large platform, he is greeted by loud clapping and the flashing of cameras. The Pope returns the greetings with a wave of his hand, and then he sits in a chair. He is usually dressed simply, in a white robe, with

▲   *Pope John Paul II is so popular with visiting pilgrims that two audiences each week have to be organized. The second one takes place in Saint Peter's Church.*

The Pope's audience hall was built by Pope Paul VI in the late 1960s so that His Holiness and the people could have a clear view of each other. ▼

a skullcap on his head.

A priest introduces the different groups of visitors to him. As each group is mentioned by name, its members stand up and cheer. Sometimes they clap or shout *"Viva Il Papa,"* "Long live the Pope!"Visiting choirs sing hymns or folk songs from their own country. Some wave flags or banners.

The Pope waves back at each group. Then he talks to them in their own language. By his side, cameramen from many different television companies film his messages. Photographers take pictures for newspapers and magazines, while Radio Vatican records his words for later broadcast on the radio.

▲ A group of newlyweds from Poland gather in the Audience Hall to meet Pope John Paul II. They are given a special place at the front of the hall.

The Pope's message

After his speeches, the Pope blesses the audience. Many people hold up religious objects to be blessed. These are usually prayer beads (called rosary beads) or holy pictures. Then the Pope steps down from the platform to meet the people. He talks to newlyweds who visit him in their wedding clothes, and he stops to bless the disabled, who have an important place at the front of the hall. Many people push forward to touch him or to give him presents from their own country.

After the audience, pilgrims can ask for a recording of the Pope's message to them at the Vatican Press Office.

The Pope is treated like a statesman or royalty. But people flock to see him because they believe that he is their spiritual leader and guide.

A group of disabled people from England wait to see ▲ the Pope. They have come to Rome on a pilgrimage organized by their local church. After his speeches, the Pope blesses each one of them in turn.

"Viva il Papa!"

The current Pope, John Paul II, is the first non-Italian to become Pope since 1523. A native of Poland, he was born Joseph Karol Wojtyla on May 18, 1920. Originally a promising young actor studying at a university in Krakow, he entered the priesthood after living through the Nazi invasion of Poland. A well-educated man, Pope John Paul II speaks 12 languages.

Saint Peter's

Saint Peter's is the biggest and probably the most famous church in the world. It stands on top of Vatican Hill, right at the end of a large square known as Saint Peter's Square.

The early church

When Saint Peter, along with many other saints, was martyred in A.D. 67, his remains were buried nearby.

About 100 years later, some Christians built a little shrine over Saint Peter's grave. Many years later, during the reign of Emperor Constantine, a huge church was built over it. Historians say it was a beautiful temple, richly decorated with frescoes, **mosaics**, and marble statues. In the middle of the 15th century, this great church was torn down to make way for a new one. Many people were angry because so many priceless works of art were also destroyed.

The new Saint Peter's

The present church was started in 1495. It took nearly 200 years to complete and cost an estimated $1 billion. Built in the shape of a cross, the church is 610 feet long and 390 feet high.

▲ *The front of Saint Peter's Church is the best-known example of Renaissance architecture. The obelisk in the center was brought there from the city of Heliopolis in Egypt.*

A special team of workmen, known as the Sanpietrini, look after Saint Peter's Dome. This massive dome measures 138 feet across. Many people think that it is the sculptor Michelangelo's greatest work. ▼

Its front door faces the rising sun, like the temples of ancient Greece and Rome. According to some writers, the early leaders of the church were not happy about this. They felt that it reminded people of the worship of the old Roman gods. But the door was never moved.

Inside the church there are many works of art, as well as altars, or special tables, where Catholic priests from all over the world come to celebrate **mass**.

The crypt

Under the church, visitors can explore a large **crypt** where many Popes are buried. Farther below, there is a grotto, which is a room rather like a cave, where archaeologists discovered Saint Peter's tomb together with the graves of some Roman people. The archaeologists expected to find a huge golden cross and a bronze coffin inside the tomb. But they were disappointed. The treasures had been stolen by Saracen pirates, who were not Christians, many years before.

▲ The High Altar is the largest of the altars in Saint Peter's. It is positioned in the middle, just above the spot where Saint Peter is buried. Only the Pope is allowed to use it.

▲ The stained glass window behind the High Altar depicts the Holy Spirit as a dove. Most Christians believe that God is made of three persons: the Father, the Son, and the Holy Spirit.

Key words

mosaics pictures on walls or floors made from tiny pieces of colored glass, pottery, or stone fitted together to form an image

mass a church service in which the most important ritual in the Catholic Church is performed. Catholics are served with a little bread and wine that is the body and blood of Christ. Jesus asked the disciples at the Last Supper to perform this ritual to remind them of him and to unite them with God.

crypt a chapel, or place of worship, under - ground

The first Pope

Saint Peter was one of the 12 disciples of Jesus Christ. Originally named Simon, Jesus gave him the name Peter, which means "rock" in Greek. A Jew by birth, Peter was a fisherman. After Christ's death, Peter became the first bishop of Rome. According to tradition, Saint Peter was the first Pope of the Catholic Church. On the Church calendar, the feast day of Saint Peter is June 29.

The making of saints

Saints are people who lived according to the teachings of Jesus Christ and are therefore thought to be holy. In Rome many churches, chapels, and even streets are named after saints.

Saints each have their own day in the year when they are remembered. On these Saints' Days, special prayers are said and processions are held. Some saints are thought to help and protect certain groups of people. These saints are called patron saints and represent many different people, from musicians to motorists!

▲ Saint Peter's Square full of followers awaiting the beginning of a beatification ceremony

Saint Catherine of Siena is the Patron, or special, Saint of Italy. Her statue stands on the Via Della Conciliazione, a street at the beginning of Saint Peter's Square. ▶

SENENSIS

Saints come from all walks of life. Some came from rich and powerful families. Others lived poorly, as **monks** or **nuns** or even acrobats. There are child saints too, such as Saint Dominic Savio and Saint Maria Goretti.

Most early saints, like Saint Paul and Saint Stephen, were executed publicly for their faith. They were proclaimed saints almost immediately by their friends and followers. These saints are called martyrs. Many saints died naturally and were not properly recognized until many years after their deaths.

Saints act as examples for living Catholics, so it is important that they are worthy of their name. Today, only the Pope has the right to proclaim a saint. Creating a saint is usually a long process involving three important stages.

Servant of God

The first stage occurs when ordinary people start praying to a dead person who has led a holy life. Perhaps this person has been martyred for his or her faith or maybe one of his or her admirers has been miraculously cured of a fatal illness. The matter is brought to the attention of a local religious group, which then informs the bishop.

The bishop then starts to collect as many facts about the dead person as possible. People are asked to come forward and give information about his or her life and holy deeds. If admirers have been miraculously cured, their doctor is asked if it is true. The information is gathered and stored in a file. A copy of the file is then sent to Rome by special courier and the holy person is declared a "servant of God."

The beatification

In Rome, the file is read by a special group of people. If these people think that the holy person could become a saint, they tell the Pope. Then a long trial begins. Every part of the holy person's life is studied closely. His or her writings are read over and over again. Medical specialists are consulted to make sure that any "miracle" really did happen. When the Pope and the cardinals are satisfied that the holy person could be an example for living Catholics, he or she is beatified, or declared "blessed."

A special celebration is then held in Saint Peter's. Admirers of the "blessed" person may come to Rome to take part.

This statue of Saint Peter on the steps leading up to Saint Peter's Church shows him holding some keys. These represent the keys to the kingdom of heaven. ▼

Canonization

The last stage of the making of a saint is called "canonization." Before reaching this stage, the "blessed" person must show the people on earth another miracle as a sign that he or she is truly with God in heaven.

When this happens, the Pope declares the "blessed" person a saint. Another, grander, ceremony is performed in Saint Peter's Church or in the saint's own country. During the special mass, the Pope tells the congregation about the saint and why his or her life and death have given so much to the Church. The saint's name is added to the Church calendar so that Catholics everywhere can celebrate his or her feast day. On November 1, which is All Saints' Day, every saint is honored.

Here are some of the more well-known saints:

▲ *Adolf Kopling, a German priest, was beatified, or made blessed, on October 27, 1991. Thousands of his followers flocked to Saint Peter's Square from all over the world to take part in the ceremony.*

Mary, the mother of Jesus, has a very special place among the saints of the Church. Roman Catholics believe that she ascended to heaven body and soul. There are over 900 churches and basilicas in Rome dedicated to her.

Saint Stephen was the first Christian martyr. He was chosen to help the disciples spread the word of Christ. But he had many enemies in Jerusalem and was stoned to death by an angry mob.

Saint Paul was first known as Saul. He approved of the stoning of Stephen and witnessed the killing. Later Saul was converted to Christianity. He wrote many letters that form an important part of the New Testament in the Bible.

Saint Francis of Assisi was born in 1181. His father was a rich cloth merchant, but Francis rejected comfort and chose instead a life of prayer and poverty. He founded the order of Franciscan monks. As he loved all living creatures, he was named the Patron Saint of Ecologists in 1979.

Theresa of Lisieux was born in Alençon, France, in 1873. She became a Carmelite nun at the age of fifteen and died when she was only twenty-four. She was remarkable for her devotion to God and her patience during a lifetime of illness. Her writings were published in a book called *The Story of a Soul*. This work was a very honest account of an ordinary person's struggle with her faith. She was proclaimed a saint in 1925.

Catherine of Genoa loved working with the sick. When plague broke out in her town, she and her friends cared for the sick and dug graves for the dead with their bare hands.

▲ *Women from Korea attend the mass during the beatification of Adolf Kopling. On their way home, they might visit Kopling's grave in the German city of Cologne.*

Maximilian Kolbe was a Polish priest. During World War II he was imprisoned in a concentration camp called Auschwitz. He offered to die in the place of an escaped prisoner who had been recaptured.

▲ *As Adolf Kopling is declared "blessed," a curtain falls to reveal his portrait hanging on the front of Saint Peter's Church.*

Key words

monks a group, or order, of men who serve God all their lives. Each order has its own aims and set of rules.

nuns a group, or order, of women who serve God all their lives. Each order has its own aims and set of rules.

Saintly facts

The first American to become a saint was Elizabeth Ann Seton. She founded the Sisters of Charity, the first Catholic community in the United States.

Temples and churches

As Christianity grew stronger, more churches were built in and around Rome.

Basilicas

The larger churches are called basilicas. These were originally used as courtrooms. They were vast rectangular halls, supported on columns. During Emperor Constantine's reign they were turned into churches simply because they were big enough to hold large crowds of people. The early Christian churches were also modeled on basilicas. One of the first of these was the church of San Giovanni in Laterano, which was built in the 4th century A.D. on land given by Constantine. It was the largest and most important church in Rome for over 1,000 years.

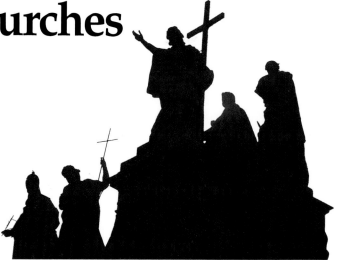

▲ The front of San Giovanni in Laterano is decorated with gigantic marble statues of Christ and the saints. They can be seen from a long distance. The church of San Giovanni in Laterano was built in the 4th century A.D. on land given by Emperor Constantine.

The church of Santi Cosma e Damiano is one of the largest basilicas in Rome. It is filled with beautiful 6th-century mosaics. Many Romans like to get married in it. ▼

Most of these early churches were decorated with beautiful mosaics. They depicted the story of Jesus and his disciples from the New Testament of the Bible. Sometimes they showed the martyrdom of the early Christians. Many of these works of art have been destroyed. But we can still see how glorious they must have been, for in churches such as Santa Costanza some of these mosaics remain.

The church of San Clemente

A lot of early Christian churches were built on the ruins of tombs or other ancient monuments to the Roman gods. No one is quite sure why. Many experts say that the early Christians wanted to wipe out all memories of the old religion. Others insist that they just wanted to use the **foundations** of these buildings because they were so solid.

One church, San Clemente in San Clemente Square, is actually built on three different sets of ruins that sit on top of each other like the layers of a cake. At the bottom are the remains of a Roman palace built in the 1st

▲ *Until the building of Saint Peter's Church, the church of Saint Paul's Outside the Walls was considered the grandest church in the world. A fire destroyed most of it in 1823 but it was rebuilt by local workers.*

The Church of San Clemente is decorated with beautiful mosaics from the 12th century. This one is placed above the altar and depicts the cross as the Tree of Life. The 12 doves represent the 12 apostles. ▼

century A.D. Above these is an underground temple built for the worship of Mithras, a Roman god. There are several sloping stones inside it. The worshipers of Mithras used to lie on these stones while eating in honor of their god.

On top of the temple sit the remains of the first church. This was built in the 4th century A.D. and is decorated with beautiful frescoes painted in 1400. The present basilica was constructed in the Middle Ages, after the fall

▲ *San Giovanni in Laterno was the first church to be built on the plan of a basilica. For hundreds of years it remained the most important church in the world; Popes were crowned there until 1870. It is also where Mussolini and Pope Pius XI signed the Lateran Treaty, which created the Vatican State.*

of the Roman Empire in Europe. This period between the 5th and the mid-15th centuries A.D. was very depressing for Rome and is often known as the Dark Ages. Many beautiful buildings were left to decay, and the people of Rome could no longer repair them.

Santa Maria Maggiore

Another well-known church is Santa Maria Maggiore. This was begun in the 5th century and shows the important position given to Mary, the mother of Jesus, by the early Christians. The church stands on the ruins of an old temple dedicated to the goddess Juno.

The Renaissance and After

After the Middle Ages came a period called the Renaissance, or rebirth. It began in the late 15th century and brought the recovery of grand art and architecture to Rome. Renaissance art was followed by a different style called Baroque, which was even more spectacular. Most churches in Rome were built in the Baroque style, which made use of plenty of space and **ornamentation**. Most famous of these are the Jesus Church, which is the head church of the Society of Jesus, or the Jesuits, and the Basilica of Saint Peter. This order of monks was created in 1534 and aimed to spread the Catholic religion throughout the world by preaching and teaching. It set up many schools and colleges, which still exist.

Pilgrims often stop to sing hymns to this statue of Mary, mother of Jesus. It stands on a column near the Spanish Steps. ▶

▲   *Inside, the church of Santa Maria Maggiore is decorated with beautiful mosaics. One of them shows Jesus and his mother, Mary, sitting side by side. This was done to show how important Mary is to Catholics.*

In other parts of Europe at this time, such as in England, the Catholic Church was no longer the only Christian church. Protestants, or people who protested against some of the grandness and wealth of the Catholic Church, set up their own churches. Protestant church architecture was much simpler and so were the services of worship.

Key words

foundation strong base on which to build something

ornamentation decorating something to make it more beautiful

Mosaics

Mosaics are an art form in which small pieces of colored glass, stone, or other material are pieced together to form a picture. These small pieces are called *tesserae*. Mosaics were created as early as 3000 B.C. by the Mesopotamians, and became very popular in Greece. The Romans copied Greek mosaics but eventually developed their own style.

City of art and architecture

The first buildings

The story of Roman art is as long and varied as the story of the city itself. When ancient Rome was still growing, its builders copied the houses of ancient Greece. Etruscan artists decorated Roman houses with **terra-cotta** statues and beautiful frescoes. Small pieces of these can still be seen in the Villa Giulia National Museum of Rome.

Julius Caesar was murdered in 44 B.C. But Emperor Augustus, who ruled between 27 B.C. and A.D. 14, carried out Caesar's plans. Many old buildings were restored, and new ones were built. Arches, columns, and statues in rare marbles and bronze graced the Forum.

By the 6th century A.D. the Forum lay in ruins. Columns and other pieces of architecture were ripped out and used later

This statue from the 3rd century A.D. shows ▲ *Christ as the good young shepherd.*

◄ *The Spanish Steps are a popular meeting place for Romans and travelers. They are called the Spanish Steps because the 17th-century Spanish Embassy to the Vatican was nearby. The church at the top of the steps is called the Trinità Dei Monti.*

As Rome grew bigger and much grander, so did its public buildings and works of art. Even many ordinary houses were decorated with elaborate mosaics, often using stone chips only .04 inches thick.

This is one of the best examples of baroque art in the world. The sculptures around the base of the obelisk (see page 38) represent earth, fire, wind, and water. Bernini was probably the first artist in the world to use running water as an important part of his sculptures. ▶

Julius Caesar's plans for the Roman Forum

Many Roman emperors built magnificent palaces, administrative buildings, aqueducts, and bridges. Emperor Julius Caesar planned many new buildings for the Roman Forum, which was a huge market and commercial center. Surrounding it were meeting places and law courts.

to construct churches and other buildings. The beautiful marble was burned to produce lime.

Nero rebuilds Rome

Nero, who was emperor from A.D. 54 to A.D. 68, restored Rome to some of its former glory after a fire destroyed many beautiful buildings and works of art in A.D. 64. Nero blamed the Christians for starting the fire and then began the task of rebuilding Rome.

He built a massive house with a golden front to live in and also a statue of himself that stood 118 feet high. Nero put the statue by the front door of his new home, which he called the *Domus Aurea*, the Golden House. Inside it was a series of **grottoes**, all filled with monstrous stone statues. These works of art have given us the word "grotesque," which today means ugly. There were also revolving ivory ceilings in the dining rooms.

After the house was finished, Nero said that he was "at last beginning to feel like a

▲ *The bridge of Sant'Angelo was built on the remains of a bridge built by Emperor Hadrian in A.D.134. It is decorated with 12 enormous marble angels once covered in gold. These were designed by Bernini and sculpted by his students.*

human being!" All that now remains to brighten up the dark ruins of the *Domus Aurea* are the paintings of Famulus.

Diocletian takes a bath

Emperor Diocletian, who reigned between A.D. 285 and A.D. 305, built a maze of public baths big enough to hold 3,000 people at any one time.

People did not go to the baths just to wash. They went to chat with their friends and to wander around the shops, art galleries, and libraries or to work out in the exercise rooms and playing fields. Afterward, there were beautiful gardens to relax in. It was like a combination sports complex, health resort, and shopping mall.

Today, all that remains of the baths is the *Museo delle Terme*, the Museum of the Baths.

▲ *The beautiful mosaics in the church of Saint Paul Outside the Walls are a brilliant example of the Byzantine mosaics that decorated many of the early Christian basilicas.*

But the central chamber of the baths was converted into a church in the 16th century. Designed by the famous architect Michelangelo, the church of Santa Maria degli Angeli is supported by eight of the original bath's huge red granite columns.

Christian art

After Rome became a Christian city in A.D. 380, its buildings and art were shaped by Christianity. Artists' imaginations were fired by the stories from the New Testament of the Bible and the lives of the early martyrs. They also drew portraits of Jesus. In some early Christian paintings Christ is not shown as a serious-faced man with a beard, but as a young shepherd with a lamb on his shoulders (see page 34). Often in these paintings he is wearing a Roman tunic. For many years, pictures of the crucifixion were not popular, as the cross was thought to be frightening.

Michelangelo

As the Church grew richer and more powerful over the centuries, the Popes asked for many works of art to be made. They ordered the building of new churches full of mosaics and paintings as well as public fountains and statues. Pope Leo X, who reigned from 1513 to 1522, belonged to the powerful Medici family of Florence, to the

north of Rome. They were very rich, and Pope Leo and his family paid for many works of art and architecture to be carried out during this time.

In 1508, Pope Julius II asked the famous Renaissance artist, sculptor, architect, and poet Michelangelo Buonarotti to decorate the ceiling of the Sistine Chapel in the Vatican Palace. Michelangelo filled it with beautiful pictures from stories in the Bible. Some of the stories were the creation of Adam; Eve and the serpent; Noah and his ark; and the fight between David and Goliath. It took Michelangelo four years to finish the work.

In 1534, Michelangelo painted a picture called *The Last Judgment* on the altar wall of the Sistine Chapel. It is one of the largest single pictures in the world. Other famous works of his in Rome are the statue, Pietà, and the 433-foot-high dome of Saint Peter's, which he designed in 1586, and also the statue of Moses in the church of San Pietro in Vincoli. Michelangelo designed a beautiful

Michelangelo's Pietà, or Pity, is the statue of Mary holding the dead Jesus. It is considered to be one of the finest statues in the world and is the only work of art that Michelangelo ever signed. His name is carved in the hem of the Madonna's robe. ▶

▲   *A Japanese television company, Nippon TV, paid for the restoration of the beautiful frescoes on the Sistine Chapel ceilings. As layers of candle wax and dirt were cleaned off, Michelangelo's magnificent colors became as bold and bright as when they were first painted. Notice the difference between these two pictures of the ceiling.*

tomb for Pope Julius II, who died in 1513. The statue of Moses was one of the sculptures for the tomb.

Bernini

Another artist who had a great impact on Roman art was Gianlorenzo Bernini. He was a sculptor, designer, and playwright from Naples. He sculpted the bronze **canopy** of Saint Peter's and the tombs of some Popes.

In 1623, he carved a dramatic marble statue of David, which was put in the Borghese Gallery. Also in this gallery is the statue of Verità, or Truth. Bernini began sculpting this statue during the reign of Pope Urban VIII. When the Pope died and Innocent X succeeded him, Bernini had to leave his work quickly, as Pope Innocent disliked Pope Urban and anyone employed by him. Verità was never finished, although Pope Innocent soon recognized the genius of Bernini and employed him to create other works of art.

Pope Innocent X asked Bernini to sculpt a fountain in the large square called the Piazza Navona. This sculpture shows, in human form, four of the great rivers of the world: the Nile, the Ganges, the Danube, and the Plate (see page 38).

Modern art

The Catholic Church still continues to encourage artists and to ask them to paint and sculpt for it. Some of the works can be seen in a special room of the Vatican Museum. Here art lovers can see works by Chagall, Picasso, and Münch. None of the named artists is Roman or even Italian, but Rome encourages and attracts great artists from other countries.

Key words

terra-cotta pottery made of baked clay and sand

grottoes cavelike rooms often found underneath churches

canopy an overhead covering, a bit like a roof

Patrons

During the Renaissance, it was common for wealthy families to support one or more artists and pay them to create paintings, sculptures, music, and other types of art. This system was called patronage. It was considered an honor for a family to be patrons of famous artists.

Legends and traditions

Like many old cities, Rome is full of interesting legends and traditions. Some of them are as old as the city itself, while others have been introduced fairly recently.

The obelisks

The ancient Romans started the tradition of decorating the city's squares with obelisks. These are tall stones, shaped like a needle with a pointed top. The Romans first saw them in Egypt. They transported them home and stood them up in the squares and important buildings. Today, only thirteen of these obelisks remain. The grandest one, the *Obelisco Vaticano*, has a famous legend:

The Pope listens to a brave sailor

In 1586, Pope Sixtus V decided to have this obelisk moved to Saint Peter's Square. The magnificent stone had originally come from the city of Heliopolis in ancient Egypt. For many years, it had stood in Nero's Circus where Saint Peter was killed. Now the Pope wanted it set up in front of Saint Peter's Church as a **relic**.

A man named Domenico Fontana was asked to move it. This was a very heavy and difficult job. Fontana hired 900 men, 150 horses, and 47 cranes. He drew complicated plans and discussed them with the Pope.

On the day the obelisk was to be moved, a huge crowd gathered in Saint Peter's Square. Pope Sixtus forbade any of the onlookers to talk during the operation. He wanted to make sure the workers could hear Fontana's orders.

The precious obelisk was carried along Saint Peter's Square. Slowly and carefully it was hauled upright. But suddenly the short ropes under it tightened. The crowd gasped. The obelisk was in danger of falling over. What could the workers do? From the crowd there came a voice. "Put water on the ropes,"

▲ *The obelisk in the Piazza Navona is called the Obelisco Agonale and is part of Bernini's famous Fountain of the Four Rivers. The Emperor Domitian had the obelisk built in A.D. 81. It is covered in hieroglyphics, an ancient way of writing, showing Egyptian gods praising the Roman emperors.*

shouted a brave sailor from the town of Bordighera who knew that this would help the ropes to hold the obelisk straight.

Pope Sixtus did not punish him for not obeying his orders. Instead he rewarded him by allowing his village to supply the palm fronds to the Vatican for **Palm Sunday** celebrations.

Coins in the fountains

Another popular Roman tradition is that of throwing coins into fountains for good luck. Coins are also thrown onto the pillars in the Roman Forum and into an unused well at the back of the church of San Clemente.

Scala Santa

Many relics, such as the Scala Santa, did not come from Rome, but were brought to the holy city from far-off lands. They were taken from wherever Christ's disciples and teachers had gone to spread the word of God. Pontius Pilate was the Roman governor of Judea who had Jesus put to death. The Scala Santa is the legendary flight of stairs from Pilate's palace in Jerusalem. Because Jesus climbed these steps on his way to the crucifixion, they are considered to be a holy relic. Saint Helena, mother of Emperor Constantine, had the stairs transported to Rome on a ship. Pilgrims walk up them on their knees as a sign of **penance** for their sins and as a sign of respect.

Martin Luther was a German priest who challenged many beliefs and practices of the Catholic Church in the 16th century. Once, when he visited Rome, he began to climb the stairs on his knees like everyone else. But then, suddenly, he stood up and walked, not in defiance of God but of the Catholic Church.

▲　*Pilgrims and tourists gather at the church of Santa Maria in Cosmedin to look at La Bocca della Verità, the "Mouth of Truth." Legend has it that if you put your hand in and tell a lie, the monster will bite off your fingers!*

At the top of the stairs is a little chapel called the Sancta Sanctorum. Through the closed gate there is a portrait of Jesus that is said to have been painted by angels.

Saint Helena also found the actual cross on which Jesus was crucified. Splinters of it are said to be hidden at the top of Saint Peter's Dome and in other places around Rome.

Tourists and pilgrims throw coins into the famous Trevi Fountain and wish that one day they will return to Rome.▼

Key words

relic pieces of bones or belongings of a sacred person, usually a saint, or things that they touched, and are now thought to be holy

Palm Sunday the Sunday before Christ's crucifixion, when he rode through the streets of Jerusalem on a donkey and crowds waved palms in celebration

penance a punishment to show how sorry a person is for his or her sins

Palm Sunday

Pope Sixtus bestowed a great honor on the sailor who saved the obelisk by allowing his home village to supply fronds for Palm Sunday. On this day people in Rome wave palm fronds in celebration of the time Jesus entered Jerusalem.

Festivals and ceremonies

▲ *On Palm Sunday, people carry palm leaves around the streets of Rome. The palms are later burned so that the ashes can be used in the "Ash Wednesday" ceremony the following year.*

The major Christian festivals

The joy of Palm Sunday, when Jesus rode triumphantly through the streets of Jerusalem; the sadness of Good Friday, when he was hung on a wooden cross; and the glory of his rising from the dead are beautifully and passionately celebrated in the churches and on the streets of Rome every year. In March or April, during springtime, the churches at these Eastertide ceremonies are full of flowers. Thousands of visitors join the people of Rome at services held in churches all over the city. But it is the Pope who draws the crowds as he gives his Easter blessing to the whole world and performs other ceremonies during this Holy Week.

Throughout the rest of the year there are other festivals, some quite small, and others, such as Christmas, which affect most of Rome. There is Carnival, when in some parts of the city people parade through the streets to mark the day before the period of Lent, during which some devout Christians choose to fast. Every church or chapel that is dedicated to a particular saint celebrates the saint's special day each year.

Smaller festivals throughout the year

On January 6, Christians celebrate Epiphany. This is when three wise kings reached Bethlehem to worship the newborn baby Jesus. Every year on the night before Epiphany, in the Piazza Navona, a toy fair is held. Children read aloud short poems in front of the statue of the Miraculous Baby in the church of Santa Maria in Aracoeli. They make a lot of noise, so that *Befana* will not forget to come and bring gifts. Legend has it that she was too busy to bring gifts to Jesus, so each year she looks for him at every house.

Saint Agnes was martyred in A.D. 304 on the place where her church in the Piazza Navona now stands. On her feast day of January 21 each year, two lambs adorned with flowers are blessed at the altar of Saint Agnes's Church. They are then taken to the Pope to be blessed again before they are sent to the nuns of Santa Cecilia in Trastevere, one of the districts in Rome. There, the lambswool is woven into special cloths that are kept in a casket at Saint Peter's.

Christmas is a very special time in Rome. Children go around the city to see the many beautiful Nativity scenes. A midnight mass is held in Saint Peter's. It is so popular that people need tickets to get in. ▼

▲ *Easter Sunday celebrates the day of Jesus Christ's resurrection, when he rose from the dead. It is the most important date in the Christian calendar. The Pope celebrates a special mass on the steps of Saint Peter's.*

On the eve of the Feast of Saint John the Baptist on June 23, the neighborhood of San Giovanni (Saint John) comes alive with a festival that involves a lot of joyful eating and drinking. The traditional food is stewed snails and roast suckling pig. By contrast, June 29 marks the Feast of Saint Peter, the Patron Saint of Rome. It is marked by very devout ceremonies in the basilica, which is brilliantly lit.

The Trastevere district of Rome is a maze of tiny streets and piazzas and the home of a very distinct and proud people. In the Middle Ages, the rest of Rome's citizens treated the Trasteverini people as outsiders. They had to fight for their neighborhood to be recognized as an official district, or *rione,* of Rome. In mid July, the Trasteverini hold a festival known as the Festa di Noanti, which is a display of Rome's varied past. Religious processions travel through the streets, where pavements are packed with people who have come to see the stalls of the street fair. At the same time, musicians play traditional Roman music.

August 5 is the Feast of the Madonna of the Snow. This day is marked by a special mass in the basilica of Santa Maria Maggiore. During the service, rose petals are thrown to represent the miracle of an August snowfall in the 4th century A.D. Pope Liberius had seen a vision of Jesus' mother, Mary, through

the snow. Where the flakes fell showed the spot where the church was to be built. The present basilica stands close to the original site.

There is one small but very moving ceremony that occurs in Rome every day. Each evening at sunset, the vesper bells in all the churches ring out to mark the end of the day and the beginning of another night.

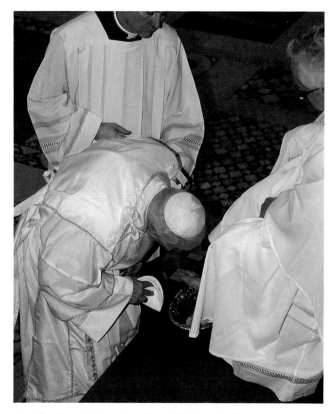

▲ *On the night before Good Friday the Pope washes the feet of 12 of his faithful. This act of humility is done in imitation of Jesus, who washed the feet of his apostles before the Last Supper.*

Befana

Just as American children wait for Santa Claus to come on Christmas Eve, Italian children wait for Befana. According to Italian legend, Befana climbs down the chimney on the eve of Epiphany. In one hand she carries a bell, which she rings to announce her arrival. In the other hand she holds either a gift, which she gives to good children, or a switch, which she uses to whip naughty children.

An open window

For nearly 2,000 years the Roman Catholic Church was very inward looking. Most of the Popes never left the Vatican after their election. Pope Leo XIII, for example, used to look at the outside world only through a closed window.

But since the 1960s, the Church has started to make links with many other faiths. During the General Council of Bishops in 1962, Pope John XXIII said that the Church needed to let in some fresh air. He called the Council "Opening a Window."

The bishops who gathered at the Council were from all the corners of the earth. Their first act was to send a message to the world. The message said that all people are brothers and sisters, whatever their race or religion.

After the Vatican Council, Pope Paul VI,

▲　Pope John XXIII is being carried on a portable throne under a canopy. He is on his way to open the Second Vatican Council. Compare this photograph with the one on the right of Pope John Paul II. What are the differences between the Popes in these two pictures?

A group of people from the Philippines listens to the Pope's Sunday message in Saint Peter's Square. The Philippines is the only Catholic country in Asia. ▼

When visiting other countries, Pope John Paul II travels in his own special car called the "popemobile." After someone tried to kill him in 1981, the Pope's advisers insisted that he should keep behind the special bullet-proof glass of the vehicle. ▲

The mass unites Catholics with each other and with God. This mass in Saint Peter's Square unites people from many countries into a worldwide community. ▼

who succeeded John XXIII, set up two organizations. One was created to make contact with different Christian churches. The other was created to open discussions with people of other religions.

In 1968 the Pope traveled to New York and made a famous speech for world peace at the headquarters of the United Nations. He also visited every continent to meet people and leaders of different countries and religions.

In Jerusalem he met Patriarch Athenagoras, who was the head of the Orthodox churches. They discussed unity between the two churches. After so many years of bitterness and division, Pope Paul VI called the Orthodox Church and the Anglican Church in Britain "sister churches."

The present Pope, John Paul II, continues Paul VI's work. He has traveled to many countries, including the United States, Brazil, Zaire, Cameroon, and his native country, Poland. In 1984 he visited England and prayed with the Archbishop of Canterbury.

He also visited a synagogue in Rome. There he referred to the Jews as "our older brothers in faith." John Paul at last began to restore good relations between the Catholic Church and the Jewish community, which had been broken in the 13th century.

In 1989 the Pope led a "World Day for Peace" in the little Italian town of Assisi. There were representatives from every major religion in the world, including Hindus, Muslims, Buddhists, and Jews. Since then this event has been repeated each year in different parts of the world. In 1991 it was held on the tiny island of Malta in the Mediterranean. The theme was "Peace in the Mediterranean."

The greatest religious building to have been constructed in Rome in recent years is

▲ All the Catholic religious orders have their centers in Rome. Nuns, priests, and monks from all over the world visit them each year.

◀ This is Rome's first mosque, which serves the city's 60,000 Muslims and the many Muslim visitors who come to Rome each year. It is made up of 16 small domes clustered around a huge central one.

not a place for Christian worship at all. In 1991, Rome's first mosque was completed, except for the **minaret**, which was still being designed.

The idea of the "open window" seems to have spread throughout Rome. It seems to have opened up people's minds to reach out to those of different faiths.

People of all religions are attracted to Rome because of its history. Here Roman, Renaissance, and holy statues rub shoulders on a souvenir stall. ▼

Key words

minaret the Mosque tower from which Muslims are called to prayer

World religions

The Roman Catholic Church is the largest in the world, with about 995,780,000 members. Recently, Pope John Paul II has urged the Church to recognize other world religions, including 935,000,000 Muslims, 705,000,000 Hindus, 363,290,000 Protestants, 303,000,000 Buddhists, 92,012,000 people practicing traditional tribal religions, 72,980,000 Anglicans, and 17,400,000 Jews.

Important events in the history of Rome

The following are some important events with the dates on which they occurred:

753 B.C.	The legendary founding of Rome by Romulus
600 B.C.	The Etruscans come from Tuscany to found Rome
509 B.C.	The Etruscans are driven out of Rome
400 B.C.	Rome builds military roads and sets up military communities to help it to control its territory in Italy
312 B.C.	The first aqueduct is built
250 B.C.	Rome gains control of the whole of Italy
133 B.C.	Rome controls all the lands around the Mediterranean Sea except for Egypt
45 B.C.	Julius Caesar becomes emperor of Rome
30 B.C.	Many important Roman writers flourished – Virgil, Ovid
A.D. 50	The population of Rome reaches one million
A.D. 54	The persecution of Christians begins
A.D. 67	Saint Paul is martyred
A.D. 80	The Colosseum is opened
A.D. 95	The Roman Empire reaches its height, with Rome as its center
A.D. 204-300	The Roman Empire is divided into an eastern part and a western part
A.D. 313	Emperor Constantine allows Christians to worship openly
A.D. 325	Building starts on the first Saint Peter's Church
A.D. 330	The Empire is reunited but Emperor Constantine moves to Byzantium and builds a new capital, Constantinople
409	Rome is invaded by the Visigoths and the Empire's decline begins
609	The Pantheon is made into a church
1000-1300	Rome slumps into ruin and decay – the Dark Ages
1450	Rome moves out of the Dark Ages and into an age of rebirth, or Renaissance
1499	Michelangelo carves the Pietà; the rebirth or Renaissance in Rome really begins
1508-1512	Michelangelo paints the Sistine Chapel
1626	Pope Urbanus VIII blesses the new Saint Peter's Church
1797	Napoleon captures Rome and proclaims a new republic and the Pope loses his power
1869	The First Vatican Council
1870	Italian nationalists storm Rome and make it capital of a united Italy
1922	Mussolini marches on Rome and takes over Italy
1929	The independent Vatican State is founded
1933	The Church loses all official political influence in Rome and Italy
1958	The election of Pope John XXIII
1962-1965	The Second Vatican Council
1963	Paul VI becomes Pope
1978	First Polish Pope, John Paul II, is elected

Further Reading

Angilillo, Barbara W. *Italy*. Austin, Texas: Steck-Vaughn, 1990.

Bonomi, Kathryn. *Italy*. New York: Chelsea House, 1991.

Coote, Roger. *Roman Cities*. New York: Franklin Watts, 1990.

Mariella, Cinzia. *Passport to Italy*. New York: Franklin Watts, 1990.

Stein, R. Conrad. *Italy*. Chicago: Childrens Press, 1983.

Index